THE PRODIGAL SON

MY MEMOIR

By Benjamin H. Liles

THE PRODIGAL SON: MY MEMOIR

Copyright © 2018 by Benjamin H. Liles

All Scripture quotations, unless otherwise indicated, are taken from the New Living Translation®, NLT®. Copyright 2007, 2004, 1996 by Tyndale House Foundation.

All rights reserved. No part of this publication may be reproduced, stored in a retrieval system, or transmitted in any form or by any means—electronic, mechanical, photocopy, recording, or any other—except for brief quotations in printed reviews, without the prior permission of the publisher.

Interior design by Benjamin H. Liles

Library of Congress Cataloging-in-Publication Data

Liles, Benjamin H.
    The Prodigal Son: My Memoir / Benjamin H. Liles.
      p. cm.
    ISBN-13: 978-1-7237-4648-0 (soft-cover: print-paper)
    ISBN-10: 1-72-374-6480 (soft-cover: print-paper)
    1. Christian Life—Non-Fiction.
    2. Memoir—Non-Fiction.
    3. Relationship—Non-Fiction.
    I. Title
  813'.54

Published in 2018

Printed in the United States of America

DEDICATION

To Jesus Christ,

Who accepts the prodigal back into His arms

And Tanya Liles,

My lovely bride and wife whom I adore immensely and with

all of my heart.

Table of Contents

Acknowledgements v

Bible Text Used vii

Introduction xiii

1 The righteous and the unrighteous 16

2 In search of what's lost 28

3 Rejoicing over what's found 36

4 The proud son 44

5 The Unjust Steward 50

6 Lovers of Money 58

7 The Rich Man and Lazarus 64

Call to Repentance: A Prayer for Salvation 73

Notes 76

Acknowledgements

There are a number of people I wish to thanks for my being able to write and for helping me in and through the process for this book.

First off, Jesus Christ, my Lord and Savior, who enabled me with the gift of communication.

Secondly, my parents who encouraged me to keep writing poems, songs, singing, playing guitar and instilling in me a spirit that never quits.

Last, my wife who believes in me and my writing ability. Hon, you are the reason this book exists. Thanks and I love you.

Bible Text Used

Luke 15

The Parable of the Lost Sheep

[1] Then all the tax collectors and the sinners drew near to Him to hear Him. [2] And the Pharisees and scribes complained, saying, "This Man receives sinners and eats with them." [3] So He spoke this parable to them, saying:

[4] "What man of you, having a hundred sheep, if he loses one of them, does not leave the ninety-nine in the wilderness, and go after the one which is lost until he finds it? [5] And when he has found *it,* he lays *it* on his shoulders, rejoicing. [6] And when he comes home, he calls together *his* friends and neighbors, saying to them, 'Rejoice with me, for I have found my sheep which was lost!' [7] I say to you that likewise there will be more joy in heaven over one sinner who repents than over ninety-nine just persons who need no repentance.

The Parable of the Lost Coin

[8] "Or what woman, having ten silver coins, if she loses one coin, does not light a lamp, sweep the house, and search carefully until she finds *it?* [9] And when she has found *it,* she calls *her* friends and neighbors together, saying, 'Rejoice with me, for I have found the piece which I lost!' [10] Likewise, I say to you, there is joy in the presence of the angels of God over one sinner who repents."

The Parable of the Lost Son

[11] Then He said: "A certain man had two sons. [12] And the younger of them said to *his* father, 'Father, give me the portion of goods that falls *to me.*' So he divided to them *his* livelihood. [13] And not many days after, the younger son gathered all together, journeyed to a far country, and there wasted his possessions with prodigal living. [14] But when he had spent all, there arose a severe famine in that land and he began to be in want. [15] Then he went and joined himself to a citizen of that country, and he sent him into his fields to feed swine. [16] And he would gladly have filled his stomach with the pods that the swine ate, and no one gave him *anything.*

"But when he came to himself, he said, 'How many of my father's hired servants have bread enough and to spare, and I perish with hunger!
I will arise and go to my father, and will say to him, "Father, I have sinned against heaven and before you, [19] and I am no longer worthy to be called your son. Make me like one of your hired servants."'

"And he arose and came to his father. But when he was still a great way off, his father saw him and had compassion, and ran and fell on his neck and kissed him. [21] And the son said to him, 'Father, I have sinned against heaven and in your sight, and am no longer worthy to be called your son.'

[22] "But the father said to his servants, 'Bring out the best robe and put *it* on him, and put a ring on his hand and sandals on *his* feet. [23] And bring the fatted calf here and kill *it,* and let us eat and be merry; [24] for this my son was dead and is alive again; he was lost and is found.' And they began to be merry.
[25] "Now his older son was in the field. And as he came and drew near to the house, he heard music and dancing. [26] So he called one of the servants and asked what these things meant.

And he said to him, 'Your brother has come, and because he

has received him safe and sound, your father has killed the fatted calf.'

"But he was angry and would not go in. Therefore his father came out and pleaded with him. ²⁹ So he answered and said to *his* father, 'Lo, these many years I have been serving you; I never transgressed your commandment at any time; and yet you never gave me a young goat that I might make merry with my friends. ³⁰ But as soon as this son of yours came, who has devoured your livelihood with harlots, you killed the fatted calf for him.'

"And he said to him, 'Son, you are always

with me, and all that I have is yours. ³² It was right that we should make merry and be glad, for your brother was dead and is alive again, and was lost and is found.'

Luke 16

The Parable of the Unjust Steward

¹ He also said to His disciples: "There was a certain rich man who had a steward, and an accusation was brought to him that this man was wasting his goods. ² So he called him and said to him, 'What is this I hear about you? Give an account of your stewardship, for you can no longer be steward.'

³ "Then the steward said within himself, 'What shall I do? For my master is taking the stewardship away from me. I cannot dig; I am ashamed to beg. ⁴ I have resolved what to do, that when I am put out of the stewardship, they may receive me into their houses.'

⁵ "So he called every one of his master's debtors to *him,* and said to the first, 'How much do you owe my master?' ⁶ And he said, 'A hundred measures of oil.' So he said to him, 'Take your bill, and sit down quickly and write fifty.' ⁷ Then he said to another, 'And how much do you owe?' So he said, 'A hundred

measures of wheat.' And he said to him, 'Take your bill, and write eighty.' [8] So the master commended the unjust steward because he had dealt shrewdly. For the sons of this world are shrewder in their generation than the sons of light.

[9] "And I say to you, make friends for yourselves by unrighteous mammon, that when you fail, they may receive you into an everlasting home. [10] He who *is* faithful in *what is* least is faithful also in much; and he who is unjust in *what is* least is unjust also in much. [11] Therefore if you have not been faithful in the unrighteous mammon, who will commit to your trust the true *riches?* [12] And if you have not been faithful in what is another man's, who will give you what is your own?

[13] "No servant can serve two masters; for either he will hate the one and love the other, or else he will be loyal to the one and despise the other. You cannot serve God and mammon."

The Law, the Prophets, and the Kingdom

[14] Now the Pharisees, who were lovers of money, also heard all these things, and they derided Him. [15] And He said to them, "You are those who justify yourselves before men, but God knows your hearts. For what is highly esteemed among men is an abomination in the sight of God.

[16] "The law and the prophets *were* until John. Since that time the kingdom of God has been preached, and everyone is pressing into it. [17] And it is easier for heaven and earth to pass away than for one letter of the law to fail.
[18] "Whoever divorces his life and marries another commits adultery; and whoever marries her who is divorced from *her* husband commits adultery.

The Rich Man and Lazarus

[19] "There was a certain rich man who was clothed in purple and fine linen and fared sumptuously every day. [20] But there was a certain beggar named Lazarus, full of sores, who was

laid at his gate, ²¹ desiring to be fed with the crumbs which fell from the rich man's table. Moreover the dogs came and licked his sores. ²² So it was that the beggar died, and was carried by the angels to Abraham's bosom. The rich man also died and was buried. ²³ And being in torments in Hades, he lifted up his eyes and saw Abraham afar off, and Lazarus in his bosom.

²⁴ "Then he cried and said, 'Father Abraham, have mercy on me, and send Lazarus that he may dip the tip of his finger in water and cool my tongue; for I am tormented in this flame.' ²⁵ But Abraham said, 'Son, remember that in your lifetime you received your good things, and likewise Lazarus evil things; but now he is comforted and you are tormented. ²⁶ And besides all this, between us and you there is a great gulf fixed, so that those who want to pass from here to you cannot, nor can those from there pass to us.'
²⁷ "Then he said, 'I beg you therefore, father, that you would send him to my father's house, ²⁸ for I have five brothers, that he may testify to them, lest they also come to this place of torment.' ²⁹ Abraham said to him, 'They have Moses and the prophets; let them hear them.' ³⁰ And he said, 'No, father Abraham; but if one goes to them from the dead, they will repent.' ³¹ But he said to him, 'If they do not hear Moses and the prophets, neither will they be persuaded though one rise from the dead.'"

Introduction

In the passages I am using I will draw my own story from them to illustrate the Father's love through Jesus Christ to humanity in order to show that we have and seen the testimony of whom Jesus is; the only begotten Son of God. It is with this knowledge that men, women, children and the elderly will have no excuse come the day the Lord, Jesus Christ, returns in glory on the clouds. For in those days, everyone will mourn His coming. I don't say these words to disprove why Jesus came, "For God did not send His Son into the world to condemn the world, but that the world through Him might be saved [1]," but the truth is that many people will stand condemned as they are because they refused to come and see that, indeed, the Lord is good.

    He endured suffering, pain and humiliation so that when we come to Him we won't endure all of that for long. God isn't slow where it concerns His fulfillment of His word, but He allows everything to happen in order so that His word may be fulfilled. "My word will not return to me void." Christ came the first time to suffer and to be crucified for our sins and of ourselves so that when we look to Him we don't pity Him being there, but seeing that we can cast our cares, hurts and sufferings there. Sure, some people look at Him on the cross and pity and despise Him, but that is their lot; that is why they stand condemned; for they saw Him fulfill the very word of the Father and yet did not cast their imperfections upon a fully unblemished, perfect lamb at His altar.

They looked at the laws of God, which were given to Moses and especially in regards to the sacrifice for atonement of sins to having broken the laws refused to put their hands on their sacrifices showing they acknowledged their sins. This is the Old Testament prophecy of what men were to do when, in the New Testament, Christ would come to put an end to daily sacrifices for good. Men were to lay their hands on His head, acknowledge their sins and then turn from that lifestyle of sinning and murder. This is why it is said that, "What purpose then *does* the law *serve?* It was added because of transgressions, till the Seed should come to whom the promise was made; *and it was* appointed through angels by the hand of a mediator…Therefore the law was our tutor *to bring us* to Christ, that we might be justified by faith. But after faith has come, we are no longer under a tutor [2]."

The law teaches us we have broken His commandments, which were given in order that we may have life, but as Paul says, "For Moses writes about the righteousness which is of the law, *"The man who does those things shall live by them."* For *"whoever calls on the name of the LORD shall be saved* [3]*."*

But, God, through His Spirit, also reveals to Paul this: "How then shall they call on Him in whom they have not believed? And how shall they believe in Him of whom they have not heard? And how shall they hear without a preacher... *But to Israel he says: "All day long I have stretched out my hands to a disobedient and contrary people* [4]*."*

In short order, we see that where the Law came to give us life in the Father, it produced death, as sin seized the opportunity once it was given to do that which was wrong. Where the Law said, "Do not commit murder," sin hated another person without cause. Christ said, "Even by hating your brother you have committed murder." There is then life when we believe that because Christ came to fulfill what was written, we are given - as in marriage – to Him, as through Christ we find life; whereas, the Law finds us guilty and death reigns in us until we have that freedom in Christ.

This is then what this story is about: though my life illustrates the meaning and the power of what these parables mean. Also, with the parable of the unjust steward, we can also be seen as unjust stewards as well. We don't have an excuse before Him, so in this manner will what can be seen in my life show that it's not only for a select type of person, but for all people. I also know that not everyone came from a good home, but if you truly see what I'm saying with my own story, you'll see that even the Lord, Christ, is better than even our own earthly, biological fathers.

1 The righteous and the unrighteous

"Now the tax collectors and sinners were all gathering around to hear Jesus. But the Pharisees and the teachers of the law muttered, 'This man welcomes sinners and eats with them.'" [5]

"On hearing this, Jesus said, 'It is not the healthy who need a doctor, but the sick. I have not come to call the righteous, but the sinners.'" [6]

"On hearing this, Jesus said to them, 'It is not the healthy who need a doctor, but the sick. I have not come to call the righteous, but sinners.' [7]

"Jesus answered them, "It is not the healthy who need a doctor, but the sick." [8]

Imagine this, the religious leaders of Jesus' day keeping their hollow traditions and truly exceptional laws from being broken that the needs of the people aren't being met. I mean, it should be noted these men are the most learned men of all Israel and they lay the laws of God as burdens down on their family and neighbors to keep and fulfill. It's an impossible task to even do. So, this is the atmosphere Jesus is in when the Pharisees and other leaders try to trap Jesus.

They have seen Jesus, known who he was and was about daily for maybe about a year or so when this chapter opens. They have a charge against Jesus claiming that he welcomes, sits and eats with sinners and yet they know this man – Jesus – has not once sinned. It makes me wonder just how truly righteous and disease free these men are.

Can you imagine someone being so holy and so pure in their own imaginations that they neglect others and their needs daily while going on in implementing their own ideas, theology and laws on others that no one can possibly keep? Of course, they see Jesus and know he's kept all of God's word so far because he trumps their every charge and levels their accusations back at them, while still being very loving and gracious to them.

Maybe that's what they have a problem with, really. They want a man, the man scriptures declare where God sends His Son to judge and rule the nations with an iron rod and a scepter. We've all been there with our own ideas and beliefs. We long for everyone to agree with us and to do things our way, but how selfish and self-serving is this idea?

While I can assume and guess away what all these men were doing in Jesus' day, we have scripture and Jesus' words showing us exactly what is going on. It is the basis for the rest of this writing. These men are so above the so-called "sinners" that they neglect their own need and sinfulness to allow Jesus the right to challenge their views.

Many men and women were challenged by this Jesus character. They see him as a problem, an enigma, a problem. He threatens their status quo, their positions of authority and their popularity with the people. They want what Jesus has; they despise him because this man, Jesus, works miracles, talks as if he sees God face to face, and walks in God's statutes. They have a problem with him, specifically for this reason.

THE PRODIGAL SON

Jesus challenges them consistently and daily that he indeed is the messiah scriptures declare him to be. I can list a dozen or more of the verses that Jesus Christ – in Hebrew his name is Yeshua Hamashiach (Jesus the Messiah) – truly did fulfill. These men have known Jesus for a long time, and who can say just how truly long that is. What we can say for certain is they despised him so much they had to mutter under their breath what he was doing.

What did it matter anyway? So, Jesus healed the sick on a Saturday, ate with sinners, drank wine with them, danced and cried as well. We have a word for fellows like this in today's culture: these men who despise Jesus and his message are religious zealots who misuse and misappropriate God's words for their benefit.

It hurts when you read scripture from the Old Testament knowing that a suffering messiah may come to confront your ways, your lifestyle, and how you teach others what God's word says. God's word isn't up to what we say it is, it is God's word, meant for us to see how much we sinned and fallen short of His glory. Certainly these men knew they would get the reminder that "if you do warn the wicked person to turn from their ways and they do not do so, they will die for their sin, though you yourself will be saved [9]."

Jesus spent a lot of time healing the people, bringing them out of sickness and disease; he opened ears, loosed tongues and still yet the people chose to ignore him and chose to side with their religious leaders. Why?

Scriptures declare they "despised and rejected," made him to "suffer" and for him to become "familiar with pain. Like one from whom people hide their faces he was despised, and we held him in low esteem [10]."

Why would Jesus do this for these people who were so obstinate, so rebellious to him and to God, the Father, knowing they were so stiff-necked? Even the scriptures from the Old Testament say that "Blessed are you, O Israel! Who is like you, a people saved by the LORD? He is your shield and helper and your glorious sword. Your enemies will cower before you, and you will trample down their high places [11]."

    Yet, these leaders, the men who were to be watchmen and watchtowers of Israel never declared a word of God to the people. It is why when Jesus countered them, time and time again, he was saying in essence to them, "See how the faithful city has become a prostitute! She once was full of justice; righteousness used to dwell in her—but now murderers [12]!" In fact, Jesus' words concerning Jerusalem towards the close of Passover week are, "Jerusalem, Jerusalem, you who kill the prophets and stone those sent to you, how often I have longed to gather your children together, as a hen gathers her chicks under her wings, and you were not willing [13]."

    It matches the parable Jesus told all the people, from the religious leaders to the people, found in Mark 12:1-12: "Jesus then began to speak to them in parables: "A man planted a vineyard. He put a wall around it, dug a pit for the winepress and built a watchtower. Then he rented the vineyard to some farmers and moved to another place. At harvest time he sent a servant to the tenants to collect from them some of the fruit of the vineyard. But they seized him, beat him and sent him away empty-handed. Then he sent another servant to them; they struck this man on the head and treated him shamefully. He sent still another, and that one they killed. He sent many others; some of them they beat, others they killed.

THE PRODIGAL SON

"He had one left to send, a son, whom he loved. He sent him last of all, saying, 'They will respect my son.'

"But the tenants said to one another, 'This is the heir. Come, let's kill him, and the inheritance will be ours.' So they took him and killed him, and threw him out of the vineyard.

"What then will the owner of the vineyard do? He will come and kill those tenants and give the vineyard to others. Haven't you read this passage of Scripture?

"'The stone the builders rejected has become the cornerstone; the Lord has done this, and it is marvelous in our eyes'?"

"Then the chief priests, the teachers of the law and the elders looked for a way to arrest him because they knew he had spoken the parable against them. But they were afraid of the crowd; so they left him and went away."

Jesus did his best and utmost that he saw the Father asking and telling him to do. While all of it was hard to do Jesus did so in order that those who do believe in him have life and have it to the fullest. What other religion can claim this? Jesus in fact told the Samaritan woman at the well, "If you knew the gift of God and who it is that asks you for a drink, you would have asked him and he would have given you living water [14]."

Yet, the very people he came to save from sin and death heaped up trouble against him, plotted his murder, called him names, mocked him, spat upon him and yet he took it all so that when they realized their sinful behavior and actions that they could and would be forgiven by him. It's with what Jesus said, "I want you to know that the Son of Man has authority on earth to forgive sins." So he said to the paralyzed man, "Get up, take your mat and go home [15]."

What is it worth to say you believe God and yet deny His son Jesus the Christ, claiming that he had no power, that he isn't the Son of God – the Son of Man – who came, took our sins, our infirmities, all of our wickedness and sins upon himself so that when we come to him faithfully and surely that God the Father can bestow and give us eternal life? By attributing all the works Jesus did to the devil and claiming that Jesus isn't God's Son means someone is in error and it doesn't seem Jesus is false in the least bit considering he fulfilled Old Testament prophecy.

Why don't we take a look at the few here and see if Jesus Christ truly is who he claimed he is.

The Birth of Jesus – "Therefore the Lord himself shall give you a sign; Behold, a virgin shall conceive, and bear a son, and shall call his name Immanuel [16]."

The Escape to Egypt and return from Egypt – "Out of Egypt I called my son [17]."

The Butchery of Israeli Children (shortly after Jesus' birth) – "This is what the LORD says: "A voice is heard in Ramah, mourning and great weeping, Rachel weeping for her children and refusing to be comforted, because her children are no more [18]."

Jesus' maternal cousin to be born, being Elijah come again, and living in the desert [19]. "See, I will send you the prophet Elijah before that great and dreadful day of the LORD comes. A voice of one calling: "In the desert prepare the way for the LORD; make straight in the wilderness a highway for our God [20]. They replied, "He was a man with a garment of hair and with a leather belt around his waist." The king said, "That was Elijah the Tishbite [21]."

Jesus' Baptism – "Then I said, "Here I am, I have

come--it is written about me in the scroll. I desire to do your will, O my God; your law is within my heart) [22]."

Jesus' Temptations – "He humbled you, causing you to hunger and then feeding you with manna, which neither you nor your fathers had known, to teach you that man does not live on bread alone but on every word that comes from the mouth of the LORD [23]. "For he will command his angels concerning you to guard you in all your ways; they will lift you up in their hands, so that you will not strike your foot against a stone.[24]

Do not test the LORD your God as you did at Massah.[25] Then Balaam said to Balak, "Stay here beside your offering while I go aside. Perhaps the LORD will come to meet with me. Whatever he reveals to me I will tell you." Then he went off to a barren height.[26] Fear the LORD your God and serve him. Hold fast to him and take your oaths in his name [27]."

Aside from the several I've listed here, for sake of brevity I will only list two more: and they are these, Jesus' clothes are gambled for [28] as well as the fact Jesus being crucified.[29]

Now here's the clincher, who truly killed Jesus Christ if scripture declares he fulfilled the law and the prophets, from the first jot (i.e. Dotting I's) to the very last stroke of the pen (i.e. crossing t's)? If God had Jesus killed then God isn't and can't be a righteous God, according to our perception. If Jesus did so on his own volition without God being God and God also not being real it just makes Jesus a madman. How can we know for sure that Jesus Christ wasn't a madman and that God didn't kill his only son, but kept a promise so that Abraham's descendants would number more than the stars in the sky?

Yes, this is the last and final prophecy I will refer to. Many people claim they are Abraham's children, but the problem is that in order to be Abraham's child that person must love God above all things, have faith that God keeps His word to a thousand generations, believe God's word (The Bible) as infallible, Living, Water and Life Eternal.

Without further ado I give you these verses: "When Abram was ninety-nine years old, the LORD appeared to him and said, "I am God Almighty; walk before me faithfully and be blameless. Then I will make my covenant between me and you and will greatly increase your numbers."

"Abram fell facedown, and God said to him, "As for me, this is my covenant with you: You will be the father of many nations. No longer will you be called Abram; your name will be Abraham, for I have made you a father of many nations. I will make you very fruitful; I will make nations of you, and kings will come from you. I will establish my covenant as an everlasting covenant between me and you and your descendants after you for the generations to come, to be your God and the God of your descendants after you. The whole land of Canaan, where you now reside as a foreigner, I will give as an everlasting possession to you and your descendants after you; and I will be their God [30]."

"Now the LORD was gracious to Sarah as he had said, and the LORD did for Sarah what he had promised. Sarah became pregnant and bore a son to Abraham in his old age, at the very time God had promised him. Abraham gave the name Isaac to the son Sarah bore him. When his son Isaac was eight days old, Abraham circumcised him, as God commanded him. Abraham was a hundred years old when his son Isaac was born to him.

"Sarah said, "God has brought me laughter, and everyone who hears about this will laugh with me." And she added, "Who would have said to Abraham that Sarah would nurse children? Yet I have borne him a son in his old age [31]."

The promise of what God planned for the redemption of mankind happened in Abraham's life and is representative here in this verse, explicitly: "Some time later God tested Abraham. He said to him, "Abraham!"

"Here I am," he replied.

"Then God said, "Take your son, your only son, whom you love—Isaac—and go to the region of Moriah. Sacrifice him there as a burnt offering on a mountain I will show you."

"**Early the next morning Abraham got up and loaded his donkey**. He took with him two of his servants and his son Isaac. When he had cut enough wood for the burnt offering, he set out for the place God had told him about. On the third day Abraham looked up and saw the place in the distance. He said to his servants, "Stay here with the donkey while I and the boy go over there. We will worship and then we will come back to you."

"**Abraham took the wood for the burnt offering and placed it on his son Isaac, and he himself carried the fire and the knife**. As the two of them went on together, Isaac spoke up and said to his father Abraham, "Father?"

"Yes, my son?" Abraham replied.

"The fire and wood are here," Isaac said, "but where is the lamb for the burnt offering?" Abraham answered, "**God himself will provide the lamb for the burnt offering, my son**." And the two of them went on together.

When they reached the place God had told him about, **Abraham built an altar there and arranged the wood on it. He bound his son Isaac and laid him on the altar, on top of the wood. Then he reached out his hand and took the knife to slay his son**. But the angel of the LORD called out to him from heaven, "Abraham! Abraham!"

"Here I am," he replied.

"Do not lay a hand on the boy," he said. "Do not do anything to him. Now I know that you fear God, because you have not withheld from me your son, your only son."

"Abraham looked up and **there in a thicket he saw a ram caught by its horns. He went over and took the ram and sacrificed it as a burnt offering** instead of his son. So Abraham called that place **The LORD Will Provide**. And to this day it is said, "On the mountain of the LORD it will be provided."

"The angel of the LORD called to Abraham from heaven a second time and said, "**I swear by myself, declares the LORD, that because you have done this and have not withheld your son, your only son, I will surely bless you and make your descendants as numerous as the stars in the sky and as the sand on the seashore. Your descendants will take possession of the cities of their enemies, and through your offspring all nations on earth will be blessed, because you have obeyed me** [32]."

God kept His word to Abraham throughout the years, in our sinfulness, our rebelliousness and has revealed to us His intentions. I don't know about anyone else, but if He didn't see us as His children, through Abraham's faith, why would He reveal these things to us if we were just His servants? Jesus said this being the difference between being a servant and being a child, a co-heir in Christ, to God Almighty, "I no longer call you servants, because a servant does not know his master's business. Instead, I have called you friends, for everything that I learned from my Father I have made known to you [33]." So it is with God's word, the Bible, to us; He is letting us know we aren't to be called servants, hired help or even murderers against Him or His people, but in being children. It's like the Apostle Paul said, "For if, while we were God's enemies, we were reconciled to him through the death of his Son, how much more, having been reconciled, shall we be saved through his life [34]."

In conclusion on this, we can say we can know for certainty that God longs to call us His children in His word, but in our hard-heartedness we are so unwilling and determined to make Him a liar that He has no other choice but to treat us as servants, being tossed aside for the rightful children. This is why Jesus constantly talked with, implored with and got cross with the religious leaders of Israel. It was to let them know that the revelation of God was staring them in the face and was willing to pay the price for them and their sins.

2 In search of what's lost

"So He spoke this parable to them, saying: "What man of you, having a hundred sheep, if he loses one of them, does not leave the ninety-nine in the wilderness, and go after the one which is lost until he finds it [35]."

"Or what woman, having ten silver coins, if she loses one coin, does not light a lamp, sweep the house, and search carefully until she finds *it* [36]?"

"Then He said: "A certain man had two sons. And the younger of them said to *his* father, 'Father, give me the portion of goods that falls *to me*.' So he divided to them *his* livelihood. And not many days after, the younger son gathered all together, journeyed to a far country, and there wasted his possessions with prodigal living. But when he had spent all, there arose a severe famine in that land and he began to be in want. Then he went and joined himself to a citizen of that country, and he sent him into his fields to feed swine. And he would gladly have filled his stomach with the pods that the swine ate, and no one gave him *anything* [37]."

Anyone who has read those verses knows that Jesus is starting each parable by describing what was lost: a sheep, a coin, and a son. In each instance, for a while – until being found, appears to be dead and gone. My life has been filled with those moments even with my own dad. My dad and I are a lot alike; we're headstrong, stubborn, we get loud, we're proud men, and we both believe we're right even when we were wrong. The one thing that set the two of us apart was the fact I never fully listened to the words of wisdom and life he gave me: "Benny (he'd say that when I wasn't in trouble), don't lie to me. I want a good relationship between us."

Nine times out of ten, in my life, I did the exact opposite. And even then, he never stopped loving me. I know, I have a good dad and yet I failed to meet his standards while I lived in his household, but what he said was prudent for me so that we would have a great relationship. Yet, when I chose my own ways and lied to him I became just like that sheep, just like that coin; I was that prodigal son. I was lost until I was found; dead until I admitted I did wrong. Even in those moments I was still my stubborn, proud self. I know that not many people will have had wonderful fathers as I have, but take heart, even Jesus Christ feels the same about all of us as my dad felt towards me. He would feel, like Christ, "I have to find my missing [fill in the blank] so I can restore [fill in the blank] to its rightful position."

A coin might find its rightful place on a pedestal with other coins that once were lost. They are now all polished; shining with radiance, showing the world how much care the Master of those coins feels for them. Or consider that lost sheep, that when found, was brought back into the sheep fold with all of the others; it's Shepherd beaming over the fact his sheep was found is back in place where it would remain and stay alive. Now consider this son of this Father, though: just like him I went my own way; I demanded for my inheritance (so to speak) and cavorted, mingled, and partied (okay, so I wasn't one of those go to the nightclub and party it all night kind of guys) it all away. Even then in that state, that place, my dad still loved me. It grieves him, just like with Christ that I went astray. For a while I'm just dead and lost from my dad.

This is how the story of the prodigal son starts.

The son demands his inheritance; then he gathers up all his belongings that are his. There may be harsh words between the father and son, and then again maybe not, but we see the son has made up his mind to go away: into another country, to be less careful with his money. He spends all of what he had and because of a famine is now wasting away.

And that's the thing. Most people who strike out on their own don't necessarily have the design of "Hey, I want to go and blow all of what I have." At least, that's the part of me that thinks pragmatically. To be honest, I'm not impractical. There are times where I lack good and sound judgment. It seems that's what Jesus is getting at with this wayward child. His judgment is clouded. It's not that he's imprudent or impractical, he's making unwise decisions. Which of us doesn't do this from time to time?

We're told that he goes and finds a master to serve, as he is in such want for money, that he becomes a pig-herder. Even with this job, he considers that the pigs eat better than him, so he eats the food they have. Then we're shown something truly disgusting: no one gives him anything, even in his state of need; they just walk by and refuse to help.

I've hit bottom myself but in regards to lying. I'd tell my dad the truth when it suited me to do so, but then I'd lie and then when trouble has found and jumped on me I'd stay in trouble (having a need) but finding that I couldn't help myself out of it I'd end up looking just as bad as the prodigal son. And it is in this way I am the prodigal son. No one would help me, a liar, out of the mess I was in. Why? I believe it has something to do with not wanting to become messy, to be considered "unclean." Thing is, just as in the case of the sheep being lost as well as the coin, both the prodigal son and I would end up being found.

My dad has told me more than once in my life, "Benny, you're known by the company you keep." And the truth of that matter is when you hang out with people who leech, who help you lose what's rightfully yours, you end up realizing later the huge price you paid. I know I have come a long way since those days, but to a huge degree it sticks with me. I realize now, more than ever, if it had not been for those moments in my life I wouldn't be able to stick so close to Jesus now.

And here it is in all of its glory: the truth is no one truly will ever help someone who isn't frugal, who doesn't use wisdom to achieve more in life. The same is true in my case on lying. Who would help a liar to be honest? Only when that person admits that lying is wrong and seeks to have the wisdom to say: "Hey, I need to be honest! No one wants to deal with a dishonest person. It is to my benefit, and to my own father, when I tell the truth." Such a person who lies, as was in my case many times, rarely will find someone who will help being pointed back in the right way.

Christ isn't just telling me with these parables that I am like a lost sheep, a lost coin, or a prodigal son, but he's telling all of us. He's saying it to the Pharisees and the people of that time. Why does he teach them with parables? He does so to illustrate things of heaven but since "those who are lost" will rarely understand, he does so that when they finally have a revelation they are lost, they can then see who it is that was sent to find them; to bring them back to life.

Can someone who is proud and lost receive the wonderful and blessed things of God? Not in the slightest. We know this by the verse, which says, "this is the one to whom I will look: he who is humble and contrite in spirit and trembles at my word" (Isaiah 66:2). Paul wrote, "Do nothing out of selfish ambition or vain conceit. Rather, in humility value others above yourselves" (Philippians 2:3). It seriously doesn't look likely that the one who is proud and arrogant can receive the things of God.

Truly, every time I lied, which seems like a lifetime ago, it took my own father to show me that yes, I lied, and that for the only way for us to have a restored relationship was to admit I had a problem with lying and needed to just say, "Hey, dad, I have a problem with lying and I'd like your advice." My entire life my dad wanted my relationship with him to see eye to eye with him. It was for both of us to not just have a good, strong, and healthy relationship, but to end up being friends like we are now; to show others why I deserve a chance to be elevated.

So, when we read the words, "A widow was looking frantically for this one coin." She's looking for it, not to spend it, but to show off the fact she has this coin she loves and wants to show off. The same can be said with the lost sheep: "Hey, everyone! I found my sheep! Let's party!" In the case of the prodigal son and myself, our fathers have to run to us while we were still a ways off, kissing our cheeks fervently, crying, wanting to give us the best of their household, and proclaiming, "Here's my son who left (lied). He, who once was dead, has found life! Let's party!"

This cannot happen when what is lost refuses to be found; especially in the case of the prodigal son. He's laying there in pig slop, eating their food (or as I just re-read the verse he was close to starvation as no one was going to give him anything), forgetting he's even human. No one wants to touch or even help him. In my case, at that time, I would wallow in my lies, languishing, but no one would help me out. Not even my own father. It's disgusting when a person goes their own way, tossing what was given to them aside, being less than they were to begin with. Did the prodigal's father, just like mine, love us less? No. Far from that! The father, in both instances, can't help because neither considered the source of their actions.

When my dad told me, "Ben, I want us to have a healthy, strong, loving relationship; always be honest with me," he wasn't being harsh or rude or even demanding, but telling me how we could stay in a strong and healthy relationship. It was when I lied and refused to admit, "Dad, I need your help" that he'd get upset with me. That's what separates my dad from the father in the parable. We're not told that the prodigal's father grieved, but I doubt he was happy and partied. He may have sat there and wondered, "What happened to my son? Where is he? I long for my son to be here and for him and I to have a great relationship." In that way, God and my father are the same.

That's why my dad was often upset with me.

"Ben, why didn't you come and tell me what was

happening?"

"Because I was scared of what you'd do, dad."

Had I just told my dad the truth in those moments, he'd have been more able to advise me, for him and I to keep our relationship intact. Let's face it though, Christ was saying the same thing to the Pharisees. Let's see how that conversation may have been different.

"Hey, Jesus!"

"Yes, Simeon, son of Jonathan?"

"I feel that what I told my dad yesterday was wrong of me to do. I told him I couldn't afford to give him help like he asked."

"Well, what did you do then," Jesus asks.

"I went over and patched his roof," yells back Simeon, probably being one of the Pharisees. I bet Jesus would have rejoiced over that. But he's telling them these parables to show them that they are just in the wrong as everyone else is. What separates a Pharisee from other people? Pharisees were religious elites, thinking they had a monopoly on the truth.

Pharisees modify the laws and make it harder for anyone else to do right. For example, using my life example of lying, the law would read, "Do not lie… except when it comes to having committed adultery. Give the man a different wife since you slept with her," or even "when you do lie about something, even if you stole an item, give back a similar item, but don't make reparations in regards to the original item."

Those who knew they sinned or had some other problem would come to Christ for their healing or admit their dependence upon Him. There was a man possessed by demons in the Gadarene district and when they saw Jesus they exclaimed, "Jesus, what have you to do with us? But so that we may not be judged cast us, Legion, into that herd of pigs." Jesus obeyed and did so. The demons left the man, entered the herd of pigs and hurled themselves into the sea, thus dying. Even demons and spirits obeyed Christ, why shouldn't we?

At any rate, it benefits me when I listen and obey my father.

What he intended was for him and I to have a great, life-fulfilling relationship so I would be successful. Jesus Christ is saying the same thing here with each parable, even with the beginning of them. He's showing us that with what God, the Father, gave to Moses in regards to the Laws that when we choose to listen to His word, not fixing it to where we benefit only from that, we have our relationship to Him restored. I like what Jeremy Camp says in his song about being restored, "All this time I've wandered around | Searching for the things I'll never know | I've been searching for this answer that | Only will be found in Your love | And I feel it my heart is being mended by Your touch | And I hear it Your voice that's shown my purpose in this world | You have restored me from my feeble and broken soul."

So, what's the point of what Jesus is saying? "Let me restore you. Life is found within me. Live in my Father's words, and watch me fulfill what He's said concerning me." This is why He came. He came so that when we believe on His death and resurrection that the Father is true to what He's said. It is written, "He did not come into the world to condemn it, but to save it."

3 Rejoicing over what's found

"And when he has found *it,* he lays *it* on his shoulders, rejoicing. And when he comes home, he calls together *his* friends and neighbors, saying to them, 'Rejoice with me, for I have found my sheep which was lost!' I say to you that likewise there will be more joy in heaven over one sinner who repents than over ninety-nine just persons who need no repentance [38]."

"And when she has found *it,* she calls *her* friends and neighbors together, saying, 'Rejoice with me, for I have found the piece which I lost!' Likewise, I say to you, there is joy in the presence of the angels of God over one sinner who repents [39]."

"But when he came to himself, he said, 'How many of my father's hired servants have bread enough and to spare, and I perish with hunger! I will arise and go to my father, and will say to him, "Father, I have sinned against heaven and before you, and I am no longer worthy to be called your son. Make me like one of your hired servants."'

"And he arose and came to his father. But when he was still a great way off, his father saw him and had compassion, and ran and fell on his neck and kissed him. And the son said to him, 'Father, I have sinned against heaven and in your sight and am no longer worthy to be called your son.'

"But the father said to his servants, 'Bring out the best robe and put *it* on him, and put a ring on his hand and sandals on *his* feet. And bring the fatted calf here and kill *it,* and let us eat and be merry; for this my son was dead and is alive again; he was lost and is found.' And they began to be merry. [40]."

Christ is telling the people that the Father rejoices just like that of the shepherd, the widow and the father of the prodigal. He rejoices when what was lost is restored. It is then revived, not just being restored. The difference I see in these parables is the object: one is inanimate, and while the other two are alive – one being a sheep and the other a man – that's the only similarity they share. It is in this third parable, that of the son we see fully how revival and restoration work.

Looking to my own life on this as well, my dad would often tell me, "Now that you've been honest with me and want our relationship back as it needs to be, here is what we will do…" Christ tells us that part of being revived in His Father's kingdom is everyone to hear, "Bring out the best robe and put *it* on him, and put a ring on his hand and sandals on *his* feet. And bring the fatted calf here and kill *it,* and let us eat and be merry; for this my son was dead and is alive again; he was lost and is found." What makes revival and restoration possible? It is in repentance. Repentance in both the parable and in my life starts with the son saying to his father as well as me to my father, "Dad, I've sinned against you and am unworthy to be your son…"

It is at this point that in hearing those words, my

dad has often said to me, "Benny, what you did was wrong and I'm glad you recognize that." He then reminds me that what I've done by lying hasn't just hurt myself but undermined his authority. Ah! So, we now can see what has transpired in the events of having gone astray. By taking the authority upon myself, as did the prodigal son, and mishandling it condemns us; we then become condemned men. When having handled their authority in this manner, distorting it for our own purpose, we're not just lost but we're claiming we know better. I've heard it said about sin that "'I' can always be found in the middle of 'sin.'" And while many people won't acknowledge they sin, we all eventually admit we've mishandled the authority given to us. This is what sin is. While even I have said, "it was a mistake," is in fact more than a mistake. Mistakes can be made up for, but missing the mark of an expectation is a sin.

For those of us who have wonderful dads, we often fail to meet their expectations by simply not listening to the wisdom they give us. Some fathers may not be Christian, but they know (even to a degree) where their authority comes from; from the Lord, Jesus Christ. So, back to this point about the first part of restoration: repentance is required as without it we would come across as justifying ourselves and not admitting we did something wrong. Revival between father and son cannot take place if the he doesn't take the time to apologize for the wrong committed.

The reason for this huge look at repentance, revival and restoration is that I truly believe that, not just for myself, everyone else wants to be recognized by the Lord as Him being their Lord. I admit there was a time in my life I did not listen to Him, and it was very much like disobeying my own father.

"Benny," He'd say lovingly to me. "Do what is right and love me. Stop lying to your dad for it dishonors him and dishonors me. Before you were born, 'I AM.' 'I AM' the father of your fathers Abraham, Isaac and Jacob. Before you were born, I knew you. I planned you." I heard that within my heart and from outside of me in the still of the balmy Texas night at the age of fourteen or so. I know it was in my teens.

I remember my response too: "Who are you Lord?"

"As I said, 'I AM' the father of your fathers Abraham, Isaac and Jacob."

My heart raced while my mind stayed calm and I tried to focus. I admit I also held a fleece out to him. "If it's you, Jesus, the wind is awfully still and it's warm out here. Make the wind blow from east to west and I will now it's you." The wind did blow from east to west and I believed He was indeed talking straight to me. So I did it again: "Lord, if it's truly you, let me enter the pool and feel the water but when I come out, only let the water from my swim trunks be the moisture on the ground." Now, we all know when a person steps out of a pool of water that the ground is immediately drenched and you can see footprints and all, but the Lord only allowed the water from my bathing suit to drench the ground. While it took me many years to fully come to the Lord, He did show to me He was and is real.

He revealed Himself to me because He knew my heart wanted more in this life than mediocrity. God didn't make men to be mediocre, but having His full grace and authority. Still, it would take me another fifteen or so years to finally realize that for me to go without Him in my life was a condemnation I was heaping upon myself. His word testifies to that, and I posted it once, but I'll show it again: "And this is the condemnation, that the light has come into the world, and men loved darkness rather than light, because their deeds were evil [41]."

    I finally came to Him one night, crying in my pain and desperation, "Lord, I stand condemned! You are holy and I am impure. I cannot even stand in your presence! Save me! When I am quiet and groaning in my sins and sorrows I waste, wilt and wither, but I am parched and I'd rather be thirsty no more. I acknowledge you and that you are my Lord and Savior, Jesus Christ." In that moment I knew He heard me and took me from the condemnation of my life's deeds and moved me to inside of heaven's walls. The devil can do his best to tell me I'm not God's son, but my joy is in Him. The devil has only a short time.

    How can I be so sure that Jesus Christ is God's own and only Son?

    It is through the fact I saw myself in the mirror of God's laws. I had other gods. I bowed to myself in worship, which is what humanism is. I did not love Him. I lied to my father and my mother many times in my life, therefore disobeying and dishonoring them. I lusted in my heart for a great deal of things and not just after women. In essence, I broke all of God's laws. And since I cannot, in and of myself, save myself seeing myself in His laws as being guilty someone, something has to stand in my place for that condemnation. This is where Jesus of Nazareth came into place more than two thousand years ago. When he came into this world, he was so not of this world as he descended from His father's throne room. He came into this world to accomplish what He saw His father do. He spoke words of life and truth and by large, no one noticed him. He was given a charge just like the two criminals and fulfilled a prophecy regarding the death he'd have: "Cursed is the man who hangs on a tree." That tree Christ hung on was a cross, the most severe form of torture by Roman standard.

If it wasn't for the fact that Jesus came to be led by God through the wilderness, being tempted by the devil and triumphing over him there, healing the sick, feeding the hungry, restoring sight to the blind and calling dead men forth from out of a cave Christ would never be who he claimed he was. I mean think on this: He called forth to a dead man, Lazarus, buried in a cave and not only did death take notice, but a dead man rose. It is why when Christ was crucified, and even before that, in which He would be raised to life. John writes in his gospel, in chapter ten that, "I am the good shepherd; and I know my *sheep,* and am known by my own. As the Father knows me, even so I know the Father; and I lay down my life for the sheep. And other sheep I have which are not of this fold; them also I must bring, and they will hear my voice; and there will be one flock *and* one shepherd.

"Therefore My Father loves me, because I lay down my life that I may take it again. No one takes it from me, but I lay it down of myself. I have power to lay it down, and I have power to take it again. This command I have received from My Father [42]." Amazing! He died on a cross, and defeated death by being raised to life!

So, then this is the life a person receives when repenting of his or her sins! Because Jesus conquered death and the grave, something all of us deserve for our sins, and we put our trust in Him that He can raise us up - since we repent of our sins – this is Him reviving us. We are given a home in heaven as a result of our heartfelt, humble repentance. We are restored to our rightful place which He intended us to have! No wonder the father of the prodigal son rejoiced! His son came back home and while still a way off, the Father sees his son, runs to him, takes the son in his arms– most likely crying – and says, "Tut tut, you don't have to say a thing. I forgive you because I love you and since you're my son and not a servant, I hand to you better clothes and food to eat! Come!"

Where is condemnation in this? There is none! However, Jesus still has a parable left within this parable of the prodigal son and it is reserved for those who feel they have done no wrong.

4 The proud son

"Now his older son was in the field. And as he came and drew near to the house, he heard music and dancing. So he called one of the servants and asked what these things meant. And he said to him, 'Your brother has come, and because he has received him safe and sound, your father has killed the fatted calf.'

"But he was angry and would not go in. Therefore his father came out and pleaded with him. So he answered and said to *his* father, 'Lo, these many years I have been serving you; I never transgressed your commandment at any time; and yet you never gave me a young goat that I might make merry with my friends. But as soon as this son of yours came, who has devoured your livelihood with harlots; you killed the fatted calf for him.'

"And he said to him, 'Son, you are always with me, and all that I have is yours. It was right that we should make merry and be glad, for your brother was dead and is alive again, and was lost and is found [43].'"

While we're told that the second son is angry, and possibly feeling resentful, for not being rejoiced over for having remained with his father – having stayed faithful – we can see that the father of these men love them dearly. He comes out to his second son, and tells him, "Son, you are always with me, and all that I have is yours. It was right that we should make merry and be glad, for your brother was dead and is alive again, and was lost and is found." It's interesting that he's not upset with his son for appearing surly over the whole thing, but he might be to a degree. We're told that he pleads with his son over this state of affairs. In looking at other versions of the same verse, it is evident the father comes outside to "reason" with his son.

I can tell he loves both his sons as for one he restores the son who repented to him and if he didn't love his second son he would not have gone outside to reason with him.

What we see is that the second son is feeling hurt, is feeling all that he's done is for nothing, and that his father has overlooked his efforts for being obedient, having not gone astray. I imagine Christ is inferring that the Pharisees are like this second son, as they have done their best to be obedient to Him staying where the Father needed them to be; they are, after all, teachers of the Laws of God.

Why would they be so indifferent to the fact Jesus is doing what He sees His Father in heaven doing? From other points of scripture in the gospel record they aren't just the teachers of the law, lawyers who interpret the law, reasoning the best way to deal with law-breakers, but they are proud and stubborn, very different from those who sinned. While Christ came to bring healing to the sinner, He also was encouraging those who remained steadfast to Him. Yet, the Pharisees went a step further. Every time Jesus showed by what authority He was doing things, they sought to kill him. Why would they want to kill God's own Son? The biggest reason I see is that by large Jesus was sent to bring reconciliation between the Father and the sinner, but to also reason with those who were teaching by way of their hypocrisy.

Over and over they claimed they knew and obeyed the Laws of God, that they were true to God, and that they knew it all. Jesus told them time and time again that they were just as blind as the tax-man, the prostitute, among others. But they stayed hard of heart and wouldn't reason with Him. We're shown that maybe a handful of sincere Pharisees understood Jesus and reasoned with Him, Nicodemus being one of them;

THE PRODIGAL SON

the other Pharisee I can think of is the one who told Jesus, "You have answered correctly," in regards to the greatest commandment. Other than that, they didn't like the fact Jesus was doing right in showing them their need for the Father. They may have been faithful to God among certain things, but by large, they led astray the people.

Something God truly hates. That is then what Jesus is doing throughout all four gospel accounts. He's not just reconciling the sinners to the Father, but doing what He can to open the blind eyes of the Pharisees; he's sent to "reason" with them. The rest of the Bible points to the fact that even these days we can become Pharisaical in our ways, demanding others to a life we can't even uphold; it is hypocrisy and mediocrity at best, disallowing Christ the right to be Lord over our lives.

Back to the example of my life, when I would come back admitting to my dad that I was wrong for lying and my sister seeing I wasn't going to be punished for coming back into a right relationship with him, she would often get angry. Why? She was the good child in our house and when she did wrong she was punished. She felt it was wrong of my dad to punish her for doing wrong when my lying was worse than her wrong. Well, in God's eyes all sin is wrong. It doesn't matter if I lied and she took a ballpoint pen, which by the way would make her a thief, both of us would get the same punishment – being separated from Him relationally as well as spiritually.

So it is the same between Jesus Christ and the Pharisees. While they went through great lengths to trap Him, He would often show them where they were in the wrong; in other words, their plans to trap Him only managed for themselves to be caught. How do you catch the Son of God in sin when He's God's only and perfectly holy Son? You can't. You make yourself out to be a liar as well as murderous. It is why Jesus finally told them, "But woe to you, scribes and Pharisees, hypocrites… Therefore you are witnesses against yourselves that you are sons of those who murdered the prophets [44]." He tells them in a few verses later that, "Therefore, indeed, I send you prophets, wise men, and scribes: *some* of them you will kill and crucify, and *some* of them you will scourge in your synagogues and persecute from city to city, that on you may come all the righteous bloodshed on the earth, from the blood of righteous Abel to the blood of Zechariah, son of Berechiah, whom you murdered between the temple and the altar. Assuredly, I say to you, all these things will come upon this generation [45]."

It is the truth as well. When Abel offered up his sacrifice, Cain was found to be with jealous rage, and instead of allowing God to correct him, Cain went and murdered his brother Abel. The same thing happened with Zechariah, the son of Berechiah. He served the Lord faithfully, giving the word of the Lord to them, saying, "Why do you transgress the commandments of the LORD, so that you cannot prosper? Because you have forsaken the LORD, He also has forsaken you [46]." Jesus is telling the Pharisees that it is they who have transgressed the Laws of God as they have forsaken what He commanded. But Jesus does his best to reason with the Pharisees anyway; telling them that it would be wise for them to repent, but they refuse to do so in their hardness of heart. In this way, all of us are prodigal sons. We can claim we haven't strayed from the Lord, but that would be a lie.

By turning back to the Lord, repenting of what we've said and done, we're allowing Him to take center stage in our lives. That was the one thing the Pharisees would not do. They knew Jesus was telling them the truth, but they did not fully recognize it was He who truly was fulfilling God's word, scripture from the Old Testament. Here's another word on this subject: anyone who knows what the Laws and the Prophets say and yet do not look at the Christ who is to suffer and take the sins of the world will never truly be ready for His second coming, the final return for His throne. They become just like the father of this world: a murderer from the start and having no life in them whatsoever.

Yet, Jesus shows them love and concern for why else

THE PRODIGAL SON

would he teach all of them in parables. By His teachings and His way to reason with us he hopes that we will listen and allow Him the right to reason with us. Going back to my life example again it would look like this:

"Benjamin, son of Tommie, will you allow me a moment to reason with you?"

"Yes, Lord," I respond.

"You do realize that all the times you lie to your father you don't just sin against him but me as well."

"What do you mean, Jesus?" I ask. "Consider this: a man looks into a mirror and sees himself perfectly, and then when he leaves he forgets who he is. What has this man done wrong?" Jesus inquires of me.

"Well, since I know you mean that the mirror is your Father's word it means that when I turn away from this mirror and lie I become a liar and the truth isn't within me," I respond.

"You have answered correctly, Benjamin."

"Lord, what must I do to become right with my dad as well as the Father, who is in heaven?" I would then ask him, realizing I sinned.

"Turn from your sins, make things right with your father and then return to me so I can forgive you. I will revive you and restore you, once I know you believe in me I can save you from your sins," he tells me.

After I apologized to my dad for the last time I sinned by lying to him, I did go back to Jesus. And the conversation that took place was this:

"Lord, I apologized to my dad for sinning against him and he restored to me being his son. I desire your forgiveness for my sins and I turn away from breaking your laws and hurting you again."

"Oh, Benjamin, son of Tommie, you have done well by repenting of your sins and acknowledging that I am your Lord and Savior. The Father tells me you mean it and therefore are now a child of His. Welcome home!" He exclaims to me.

It is only after He has allowed me in to heaven, forgiving me my sins, making me His co-heir, a child of the Father that the rest of the kingdom rejoices with Him for me coming from death to life. However, some of God's people will look upon that moment and accuse Him of doing right.

To them He reasons with them, "Were you not with me from the beginning? All I have is yours as well and yet you want me to punish him when he's admitted his wrong-doing? It is right that we should make merry and be glad, for Benjamin, your brother was dead and is alive again, and was lost and is now found."

Yet, because the world hated Christ I know I will be hated too. It doesn't recognize Christ and as a result there will always be a Pharisee who says, "You know, Benjamin son of Tommie, lied to you once, what makes you think he won't do it again?" They'll wag their fingers in His face and all He'll say to them is, "Let the person who is without sin cast the blame fully on Benjamin." Even then, Christ still says more to the Pharisees regarding their hypocritical behavior.

5 The unjust steward

"He also said to His disciples: "There was a certain rich man who had a steward, and an accusation was made that this man was wasting his goods. So he called him and said to him, 'What is this I hear about you? Give an account of your stewardship, for you can no longer be steward.' Then the steward said within himself, 'What shall I do? For my master is taking the stewardship away from me. I cannot dig; I am ashamed to beg. I have resolved what to do, that when I am put out of the stewardship, they may receive me into their houses.'

"So he called every one of his master's debtors to *him,* and said to the first, 'How much do you owe my master?' And he said, 'A hundred measures of oil.' So he said to him, 'Take your bill, and sit down quickly and write fifty.' Then he said to another, 'And how much do you owe?' So he said, 'A hundred measures of wheat.' And he said to him, 'Take your bill, and write eighty.' So the master commended the unjust steward because he had dealt shrewdly. For the sons of this world are shrewder in their generation than the sons of light.

"And I say to you, make friends for yourselves by unrighteous mammon, that when you fail, they may receive you into an everlasting home. He who *is* faithful in *what is* least is faithful also in much; and he who is unjust in *what is* least is unjust also in much. Therefore if you have not been faithful in the unrighteous mammon, who will commit to your trust the true *riches?* And if you have not been faithful in what is another man's, who will give you what is your own? No servant can serve two masters; for either he will hate the one and love the other, or else he will be loyal to the one and despise the other. You cannot serve God and mammon [47]."

To be honest, in regards to my life I would say I'm not very street smart as I was raised in a good home, not a broken home. I'm not saying that a good man can't come from the streets, as Jesus lived the mean streets of Israel in His time, but I wasn't raised in that manner. It is true my dad did tell me that I needed to keep my wits about me, but what is being said about the Pharisees in these verses is that they know how to cut the angles better. However, it is in this way they are unjust. They help people cut corners, unlawfully, so that when it comes to Jesus coming back they can't justify themselves.

He's telling them here that, "So, the master praised the dishonest [unrighteous; unjust] manager for being clever [shrewd; prudent]. Yes, worldly people [L the children of this age] are more ·clever [shrewd; prudent] with their own kind [contemporaries; generation] than spiritual people [L the children of light] are.

"I tell you, make friends for yourselves using ·worldly riches [L the mammon/wealth of unrighteousness] so that when those riches ·are gone [fail; run out], you will be welcomed in ·those homes that continue forever [eternal dwellings/tents; C God's presence] [48]."

In other words, what Jesus is saying is that it is better for those of us who belong to Him to deal in a right manner regarding everyone, doing what is right. The steward who deals unjustly in the small matters will be unjust in the bigger matters. I don't think I'd want to deal with someone who would be unjust in his dealings with me, nor do I believe anyone else wants that either. Such men come to a bad end, and not just by God's standards. By serving God in dealing with other people honestly, an honest man can be promoted to bigger and better things as this man has roots in integrity. The man who serves himself, or in the case of which Christ speaks – the Bank, has little integrity and may be promoted for being shrewd in his dealings, but when he gets promoted he may not last long with bigger projects.

THE PRODIGAL SON

It doesn't work that way in God's kingdom. The just get rewarded over the unjust, for they let their light be seen by both God, first, and then to other men. They take a stand in what is noble and right. This is what Christ fully says in these verses. No one can serve God and their appetite for money; such a man will hate God and love money or love God and hate money. You just can't serve two masters. If I use my life as an example regarding this, I'd have to go back to my childhood when I was learning right from wrong. I would steal someone's toy and then claim I was taking back what was rightfully mine. In that sense I was being unjust, but it was a learning experience and I ended up being honest enough to admit I was in the wrong. I can justify my past actions for the wrong I did, but by God's law I was a thief and I did get punished for my unjust actions as well as for lying about it. All men, both male and female, will have to answer to the Father for all their actions; if they are sealed in Christ, He will cover up their sins and they have a place in His glory, but for those who seek to justify themselves, believing they have no need for Christ will be separated from His glory for all time.

These aren't just my words on the matter, but they are in God's word. We have life everlasting when we repent of our actions to Him, it is then Christ who revives and restores us. When we choose to stay in our rebellious, prideful state justifying ourselves and actions we are just like the Pharisees who moan and groan about Jesus hanging out with the sinners. We need to wake up and see we're just as bad as those Pharisees! I've done that as well and Christ isn't amused by our blatant hypocrisy! When I first came to Christ I was all about doing what "I" thought was right, and that meant making it hard on others to even find Christ. It's like me trying to make a camel fit through the eye of a needle. It can't work! Why? No one can come to Christ when they see themselves in the light of the Law and then see what all they have to do to even make things right so they can get there. It's impossible and unheard of. This is why Christ did His best to reason with the Pharisees time and time again. He was showing them that even by their standards and measurements they were guilty of everything. Still they did not recognize Him because they were blind to their own teaching.

Here's a better way to look at it all: Abraham was dead in his loins and so was Sarah in her womb, but did Abraham doubt the Lord? No, he believed that the Lord could accomplish what he said and the result was Abraham being credited with faith and righteousness. Sure, Abraham was born before the Laws of God were handed down, but God made Himself known to Abraham and Abraham listened and obeyed! This is why Christ told the Pharisees, "I know that you are Abraham's descendants, but you seek to kill me, because my word has no place in you. I speak what I have seen with My Father, and you do what you have seen with your father."

They answered and said to Him, "Abraham is our father."

Jesus said to them, "If you were Abraham's children, you would do the works of Abraham. But now you seek to kill me, a Man who has told you the truth which I heard from God. Abraham did not do this. You do the deeds of your father."

Then they said to Him, "We were not born of fornication; we have one Father—God."

Jesus said to them, "If God were your Father, you would love me, for I proceeded forth and came from God; nor have I come of myself, but He sent me. Why do you not understand my speech? You are not able to listen to my word. You are of *your* father the devil, and the desires of your father you want to do. He was a murderer from the beginning, and does not stand in the truth, because there is no truth in him. When he speaks a lie, he speaks from his own *resources,* for he is a liar and the father of it. But because I tell the truth, you do not believe me. Which of you convicts me of sin? And if I tell the truth, why do you not believe me? He who is of God hears God's words; therefore you do not hear, because you are not of God [49]."

The whole truth of the story of the prodigal and my life as well as with what Jesus reasons with the Pharisees is that seen in the light of what He's telling them is they'd have as much right to be children of Abraham; he loved God and his fellow men, never once condemning anyone to death, but having believed that he indeed would be "a father of a great multitude." Christ, who has known no sin, can judge men and their hearts according to their deeds. More often than not they condemned Him by saying He did the works He did by the power of Satan; but Satan cannot cast out himself and it is why Jesus said, "A house divided against itself cannot stand." They tell Jesus their father is Abraham, but with murder in their hearts towards Jesus who came to give life and to reason with them to turn from their ways, it seems more obvious than not that they were saying, in essence, "We know better than you do!" Jesus tells them, basically, "Because of the fact my word has no place in you, and how can you say you are a descendant of Abraham? Should God be your father you would have listened and obeyed Him from those times and even now when I speak, but you seek to destroy me. You cannot hear my voice as you are not a child of God, but that of the devil."

    This did enrage the Pharisees and for a time I thought I was of the devil myself because of how I handled God's word. In both ways, both sons of the father were prodigal; one son having demanded his own inheritance and squandering it away, the second son challenging his own father's wisdom in allowing his son back into their home to celebrate being back. The fact is God loves all of us, but if we sit there and claim we know and have seen Jesus Christ we're only deluding ourselves. The only way we can actually see Christ is by becoming like the prodigal son, coming back in repentance, being revived and then restored back into the household. A person can't be in His household by challenging God's authority on which He should show mercy and the lack thereof. This is why Jesus tells the Pharisees, "Your father is the devil." The devil seeks to accuse anyone and everyone; both the believer and non-believer.

So, how can we overcome this obstacle and being revived and restored as a child of God? First off, we can't sit in the place of authority anymore but truly and actively listen to His word. Second, by doing what His word says, "'Love the Lord your God with all your heart and all your strength and your entire mind.' This is the first and greatest commandment; the second is like it: 'Love your neighbor as yourself.'" It is of huge disservice to claim we love the Father and yet show nothing but coldness and apathy towards others. I've done it; I know what I'm saying. I'd rather what Jesus tells and shows me about who I am now to be that beacon of hope to others.

Since there is still time to encourage other prodigals to return home, that they will not be judged nor receive condemnation if they truly repent of their sins, it would make me look bad and terrible for me to say all of this and then to suddenly say, "Wait! You have still yet to do this…" All they have to do is come in humbly, repenting of what they did, which in my case was lying to and about my own dad. For years I justified myself and my anger by saying, "Oh, my dad? Yeah, he abused me." I was going to receive the condemnation on several different levels; one being for lying and thus dishonoring him, the second being for me to sit over my own dad as a judge. It's not up to me to pronounce condemnation on my dad. What I can do though is forgive my dad, as I already have, and receive from Christ a life that I don't deserve. The other thing I can do is to allow Him to heal my pain, my heart's pains, and act like His child, doing what I've seen Him do: to forgive others of their sins.

That's the wonderful gift of God as well: love covers a multitude of sins and offenses. Whatever injustice you've been through, God can justify you through your repentance. He's done so with me, and He also encouraged me, in my faith, instead of judging people too harshly, to reason with them. It is far better now that I am His child to show people why it is important to come to Christ with their wounds. If they reject the fact that Christ wants to forgive and heal them, then they stand condemned for what they refuse to receive: life everlasting. God did not plan for us to be complacent in this world to hate and murder each other, but to speak words of life and of wisdom. His wisdom is this: exalting yourself over Him who created you is a terrible thing, for you will be judged by your own standard and His as well. He doesn't bow down to us, but us to Him. That's how it will be at the end of this age as well: ALL knees will bow down before Him, both the just and the unjust.

6 Lovers of Money

"Now the Pharisees, who were lovers of money, also heard all these things, and they derided Him. And He said to them, "You are those who justify yourselves before men, but God knows your hearts. For what is highly esteemed among men is an abomination in the sight of God.

"The law and the prophets *were* until John. Since that time the kingdom of God has been preached, and everyone is pressing into it. And it is easier for heaven and earth to pass away than for one letter of the law to fail. Whoever divorces his wife and marries again commits adultery; and whoever marries her who is divorced from *her* husband commits adultery [50]."

Jesus continues on in His reasoning with the Pharisees as they are lovers of money and pleasure by condemning what they esteem in their hearts. He says here in these verses that they "justify themselves in the sight of men, but since God knows their hearts, being an abomination before the Father. What the law and the prophets said were until John the Baptist, but since that time God's kingdom having been preached, every person presses into it. It is far easier for God's creation to pass away than for the letter of the law to fail. Whosoever divorces his wife to marry a different woman commits adultery; and whosoever marries a woman who is divorced from her previous husband commits adultery." Jesus is saying all of this to show the Pharisees that while He knows their intentions and their deeds that they are indeed the very people He refers to as "hypocrites!"

The Pharisees did everything they could within the time of Jesus' ministry to disrupt God's kingdom having advanced. It was as if through all the reading and application of the Old Testament laws and prophecies went unnoticed to the Pharisees. Even though quite a number of the prophecies deal with Christ coming in full glory to subdue the nations and to set up an eternal throne, it was in the minds of those teachers of the law that Christ wouldn't be in their midst as a suffering Savior. It never quite crossed their minds that He would come the first time around to give sight to the blind, to work when He saw the Father work, and to do that which was lawful for Him to do; He is the Son of God after all.

No, the Pharisees' hearts were hardened; they fully thought they knew it all. Scripture in the New Testament claim that they continually wore their "religious" clothes in public, but their private lives were shallow. They made it a big show that they were doing right, but in fact more often than not their motives were just plain wrong. Speaking on my behalf I admit I've done the same myself, but the difference is that I truly believe that it is better for myself to do what's right all the time, not just when it suits me to do so. When my wife and I have our moments of misunderstanding, I turn myself around to admit I was wrong, and seek what I can do to show her favor and grace. "For I desire mercy and not sacrifice," His word says. In other words, if I'm trying to worship Him and I know I'm guilty of something in the like of dishonoring my parents or a grievance I have with someone, it would be in my interest to first resolve those issues so that the Lord will show me favor.

In other words, when I show His favor to someone when I know He's shown me favor, it keeps me on His good side. He'll stay open to my prayers and what my needs are. It is when I choose to be shallow and thinking I'm wise, doing what is wrong but acting all spiritual and holy that He's removed to a distant place from me. It's not because He's really that far from me, but it's me having moved about one hundred yards away from Him. That's the truth on the situation. It's like Jesus even said, "They pay me lip-service, but their deeds are known to me; they are wicked (okay, so it's a paraphrase)." Besides, it isn't up to me who can see Heaven and who can't. That's up to the individual. All I can do is to do what I know Jesus would do: help those who can't help themselves and to forgive those who either meant to hurt me or did it without knowing.

    When it comes to Christ saying, "Whoever divorces his wife and marries again commits adultery; and whoever marries her who is divorced from *her* husband commits adultery," what He's saying there is that the Pharisees truly believe they belong to God, but it is as if they committed adultery against God; for they serve themselves and not Him. Paul, in Ephesians 5, alludes to the husband as being Christ and the bride of the husband as being the Church. Looking back at what Jesus says about divorce adultery in those verses it's apparent that the Pharisees believe it's okay to divorce their people from them so they can serve themselves; but in doing so they are seen as an adulteress who has forgotten who her husband is and married another man. The Pharisees claim they "belong" to the Father, but what they believe and how they treat others is far from how the Father treats His own beloved people, and this includes those of us who are Gentile.

    So, basically what Jesus is saying of the Pharisees is, "You say you are children of the Father, but the fact is the devil is your father; you have divorced yourself from the Father, seeking pleasures for yourself than helping those you claim you love. Your hearts are far away from Him!" He's doing everything He can to reason and persuade them to consider the fact they are a proud and hypocritical bunch. I've admitted several times over I am not just a prodigal but a former Pharisee myself; Paul was of that same material I am. He knew about as much of the Law and the Prophets and in his zeal he thought he did right by the Father going after Christ's apostles. In doing so, it left him a marked man in Christ's eyes. He finally intervened and confronted Paul, asking Him, "Saul, Saul why do you persecute me?"

"Who are you, Lord?" inquires Paul (who was once Saul of Tarsus).

"I am Jesus, whom you are persecuting. It is hard for you to go your own way when I'm trying to lead you," Jesus responds.

So, Paul asks Him, while trembling in astonishment, "Lord, what do you want me to do?"

Jesus tells him to get up off the floor, go into Damascus and wait until told what to do. As there were other men with Paul, they stood speechless, having heard a voice but seeing no one. Paul arose from the ground, and when he opened his eyes was blind; so was he led into Damascus. For three days he was without sight.

For those of us who know what Acts nine is saying, Saul, while breathing out murderous threats and on his way to Damascus to imprison the believers of Christ and possibly witness their execution comes face to face with Jesus Christ who blinds him, telling him to go into Damascus and wait for Ananias to heal him of this "spiritual" blindness as well as physical. We're told Paul ate and drank nothing for those three days and that Ananias was afraid of coming to Paul to restore to him what the Lord took away: Paul's sight. Even though Ananias is afraid of Paul, he does what Jesus commands of him as Paul is, "a chosen vessel of mine to bear my name before Gentiles, kings, and the children of Israel. For I will show him how many things he must suffer for my name's sake." Ananias thus goes to Paul, restoring sight to the man, as Christ has told him to do and for Paul to be filled with Jesus' Spirit. It is only then when Paul receives sight and has a name change from Saul of Tarsus to being the Apostle Paul, servant of Jesus Christ. We're told also that once he received his sight, he got up and was baptized by Ananias and then he ate and drank and his strength was restored. Then he spent some time in Damascus with the believers there.

The point of adding Saul's confrontation and conversion with and through Christ is to show how far Jesus Christ will go, by the hands of the Father, to restore to Him those whom He planned to show the world who He truly is. While Saul's conversion is dramatic, not everyone's conversion is. Take me for example: I was a known liar for years; I was very hateful toward those who hated me, had breathed anti-Semitism for one day against two very close and dear friends – which I knew was wrong – and in the end was allowed to see what I was doing as well to Jesus Christ. He appeared to me not just once, but a couple of times, telling me that what I was doing in my life was wrong. He told me I was very much like the prodigal son, at first, having gone astray using my own father's treasures for my benefit and after having squandered what I was given, came back into his household with great joy. It was also somewhere in that time, or soon after, I started acting like the second brother, a Pharisee, arguing with God the Father about others being in the wrong, but how I wasn't. It was very hypocritical of me.

Thing is, if Jesus Christ didn't love any of us He certainly wouldn't have followed what He saw His Father to the end to where the cross stood. He allowed for Himself to take our sins upon Him and to die so that when we see how much He loved us, we can come to Him in love and cast our sins upon Him. He truly came to redeem us, even while we weren't just His enemies but also sinners who couldn't reach a Holy Father. He came so that we might have life, to have our stripes healed, to give us sight, our river that quenches our thirst and our bread so that we will never be hungry. His word is true when He says that doing the will of the Father is more important than living to fill our own stomachs, and that the Father alone can provide for us in all things.

What we need are eyes of faith, that while we may not see Him physically, we will know He is there comforting us with His love and grace; bestowing mercy on our lives; challenging us out of our mediocrity, to rise above it and to do good to others who need it as bad as we do. For when we do the good that we ought to do, in Jesus Christ as He did it first, the world can truly see we belong to Him. While we will slip up, and I can testify of this myself that I do slip up, we can also rest in the fact that He is standing there waiting to forgive us, but it is up to us to always be present before Him, performing His word as He's proclaimed to us; to love the Lord, God – the Father – with all of who we are as well as loving others as ourselves.

7 The rich man and Lazarus

"There was a certain rich man who was clothed in purple and fine linen and fared sumptuously every day. But there was a certain beggar named Lazarus, full of sores, who was laid at his gate, desiring to be fed with the crumbs which fell from the rich man's table. Moreover the dogs came and licked his sores. So it was that the beggar died, and was carried by the angels to Abraham's bosom. The rich man also died and was buried. And being in torments in Hades, he lifted up his eyes and saw Abraham afar off and Lazarus in his bosom.

"Then he cried and said, 'Father Abraham, have mercy on me, and send Lazarus that he may dip the tip of his finger in water and cool my tongue; for I am tormented in this flame.' But Abraham said, 'Son, remember that in your lifetime you received your good things, and likewise Lazarus evil things; but now he is comforted and you are tormented. And besides all this, between us and you there is a great gulf fixed, so that those who want to pass from here to you cannot, nor can those from there pass to us.'

"Then he said, 'I beg you therefore, father, that you would send him to my father's house, for I have five brothers that he may testify to them, lest they also come to this place of torment.' Abraham said to him, 'They have Moses and the prophets; let them hear them.' And he said, 'No, father Abraham; but if one goes to them from the dead, they will repent.' But he said to him, 'If they do not hear Moses and the prophets, neither will they be persuaded though one rise from the dead [51].'"

While I have said that the Law and the Prophets can show us that we can indeed have life when we practice what it says, we must be sure that we haven't just heard the words, but that we put them into practice. It's been in here once that "it is far better to practice the word, which you know. Keep yourself unspotted from the world." Well, it's phrased differently, but it is in here. The reason is that while we may think we appear religious, we only pay the Father and Christ lip-service; it makes us look hypocritical and worldly when we forget what His word says. Take for example God's word saying that since we're no longer slaves to sin we are now saints in His kingdom; however, we sure look like we're still slaves to sin when we allow worldly pleasures to entice us away from what His word says.

He tells us, "Love me as I loved you; lusting after nothing but after the things of God." Lust is a bad thing when it promotes self-desires, self-pleasure – in short, just being selfish; but we can lust after doing the right things God wants done: like lusting after each person's soul to belong to God. In this case, it isn't even lusting, but showing compassion and care for other people. When the desire to be selfish is nullified, lust is replaced by genuine concern. It shows others you're more about doing right by others, not by what's right for only you. Instead of the thought of, "Hey, it's all about me," it becomes more of, "Hey, what can I do for you?"

I tend to worry about what I can afford to pay, like bills and making sure there's food in my home and while it is somewhat healthy and normal to do that, it's not normal to excessively be all, "I need money, I need money, I need money; money, money, money!" And while I still have the potential to lie about things I realize it's better for me to stay and be honest as people like me much better when I am honest. My dad once told me, "Benny, an honest man doesn't have to remember the things he's said as they were true to begin with." While he's partially right, it's good to know what the truth is and to stand firmly on it, always declaring it. No one likes liars, especially

God. I also used to steal, but like I said, that was back in my childhood; I don't steal anymore as I'm content with what I have.

In fact, it would be wise to look at God's Ten Commandments (His laws) and see the best way we can put them into practice:

1) I *am* the LORD your God; you shall have no other gods before me. – Practiced: I love the Lord; there is no god but Him. Therefore, I will only look to Him.

2) You shall not make for yourself a carved image—any likeness *of anything* that *is* in heaven above, or that *is* in the earth beneath, or that *is* in the water under the earth; you shall not bow down to them nor serve them. – Practiced: The Lord, Jesus Christ, died on a cross and this is to where I will look; in doing this I remember that He alone is the object to whom I worship. God allowed Himself to be humbled and longs for our worship, fellowship with me, so I worship Him alone.

3) You shall not take the name of the LORD your God in vain. – Practiced: This is a harder one for me to do, but I find that when I want to say, "Holy," I usually follow up with "Heaven" or "God." For me to use "God" and an expletive, or "Holy" expletive or even "By heaven's gates" all are seen as profaning Him. It is prudent on my part to find better ways to talk when I'm either upset or excited.

4) Remember the Sabbath day, to keep it holy. - The dogmatic on this verse tell us we should rest on Saturday as it is the seventh day of the week; seventh meaning Sabbath. Sunday marks the first day of the week if you look at our calendars. – Practiced: Even when Christ worked on the Sabbath, He did so when

He saw His Father working. So, in light of this, doing right on the Sabbath is permissible as it lines up with the first three commandments – loving Him.

5) Honor your father and your mother – Practiced: When I listen to the wisdom they have for me and my life I show that I love the Lord as well as my parents. If they need help with something and I'm available to help them, then it looks better on me, as their son, to go and help them out.

6) You shall not murder; Christ amended this Law by saying, "He who hates his brother has committed murder." – Practiced: If I or my sister, or any number of my friends and I have a problem we need to seek to resolve the issue immediately. Letting my emotions get the best of me where I want harm to come to them puts me responsible if something happens to them. A perfect example was the last time I lied to my dad; after I lied to him and then admitted I did so, I think I thought, "I despise you," and when he had his heart attack I suddenly felt a deep sense of remorse. I love my father deeply and what made me feel bad was thinking harmful thoughts about him. Nevertheless, my dad forgave me and so did the Father.

7) You shall not commit adultery. This is another law/command Christ had an additional thought on: "I tell you, if you so look at a woman (or man) with lust in your heart you committed adultery." – Practiced: When I look at someone of the opposite sex it should be done out of love and care, not of selfish desire; this is what lust is. Lust is also seeing an object with selfish desire; lust and covetousness go hand in hand. Therefore, the practical side is to not hold your gaze on either male or female, which ever can lead you to temptation. "No temptation has overtaken you except such as is common to man;

but God is faithful, who will not allow you to be tempted beyond what you are able, but with the temptation will also make the way of escape, that you may be able to bear it [52]." God is faithful to us, so it is wise to be faithful to others.

8) You shall not steal. – Practiced: To me, this goes hand in hand with the previous command/law in that if you look at an object and desire it, it stands to reason to obtain it in the right manner than a taking by force; like when at the grocery store, pay for an item, just don't walk out the door with it. That just makes other people have to pay more so that the item taken is recovered; it also prevents sales associates from losing part of their paycheck.

9) You shall not bear false witness against your neighbor – Practiced: Since this goes hand in hand with "you shall not lie" on my part I will not say something untrue about someone who lives next to me or even on the next block. Slander and libel are also part of falsely accusing others. Saying something that just isn't true puts you on the hook with God.

10) You shall not covet your neighbor's house; you shall not covet your neighbor's wife, nor his male servant, nor his female servant, nor his ox, nor his donkey, nor anything that *is* your neighbor's – This is the longest command of them all as it puts all of them together. God in all of His ways made all of us, including our neighbor, and by setting our eyes on that which is not ours and envying after it breaks all the previous commands/laws. Practiced: Instead of longing for something my neighbor has or being ill-content with what I have, it is better for me to inquire of the Lord what is best. Coveting is selfishly and jealously desiring that which is not mine.

Lust falls under this category as when you look and burn for desire for his wife, let's say, you may go through all the means available to require what you selfishly desire. This was King David's downfall. He didn't just ruin his own image but also hurt God, Bathsheba and ultimately killed one of his best armed men, Uriah the Hittite.

The point to this chapter is that the rich man who begs for Abraham's help can't be helped as he rests in Hell, which is separated completely from Heaven. There is a yawning chasm that keeps those there from receiving God's help and they need to have thought of their actions before they were put in there.

This place isn't actually destined for us as God's creation, but for the angels that fell in the rebellion (this is altogether a different book).

The best way to summarize this is that it is far better to use wisely what the Father gives to us; He gives to us each what He believes we can handle. In the end we're held to account for how we used what He's given to us. I will give to Him an account of my sins and whether or not I have a relationship to His Son, Jesus Christ. Did I make it evident I belong to the Father, or to the devil? Did I witness to Jesus Christ, showing He wants to love each of us as He commanded? Did I deal fairly and honestly with everyone as Jesus did when He lived on this planet? See, while God put us here on planet Earth, it is not our permanent home. He has designed Heaven, his throne room, to be our dwelling place with Him forever. When we seek to find and obtain wisdom in our lives, and in my life it will be a constant must to do so, I will always look to His laws to – first, see if I have upheld His laws or have broken them and second, to see if my relationship to Christ has been maintained.

I can sit here and claim I belong to Christ as the day is long but if I don't show true compassion, true care and love to others as He has shown to each of us I'm not better than a sinful liar. Both that person and I will be judged for our actions as well as our lack of a relationship with Jesus Christ. That is what this book has been about. To be revived and restored to Him; to be used right in Him and reaching out to help others see the best God has to offer each and every one of us. I won't gain much in the next life if I don't show the same level of love and compassion as Jesus Christ gave to me or any of us. I may not be as finely educated as a Pastor, or even have the right words or theology, but it is Christ alone who gives me the strength and understanding of what He's saying through the Bible.

Beloved, all I know is this: He misses you and your face. He longs to wipe away your tears and call you His child. Won't you come, when you see yourself in the proper light of His word, and see you truly need Him? I cannot make you come and make a decision to belong to Christ, but I do hope I presented all of what He's put on my heart to you. Neither of us truly wants to be separated from His love for eternity.

Call to Repentance: A Prayer for Salvation

Most pastors, leaders and teachers are conventional with the scriptures they use when leading repentant people to Christ; however, I believe I serve a Savior who used unconventional methods, radical ones even to bring healing and life to them. Therefore, the verses you're about to see are so unconventional in usage:

"And it happened when He was in a certain city, that behold, a man who was full of leprosy saw Jesus; and he fell on *his* face and implored Him, saying, "Lord, if You are willing, You can make me clean." Then He put out *His* hand and touched him, saying, "I am willing; be cleansed." Immediately the leprosy left him [53]."

"Now it happened on a certain day, as He was teaching, that the Pharisees and teachers of the law sitting by, who had come out of every town of Galilee, Judea, and Jerusalem. And the power of the Lord was *present* to heal them... And they were all amazed, and they glorified God and were filled with fear, saying, "We have seen strange things today [54]!"

"So when Jesus had received the sour wine, He said, "It is finished!" And bowing His head, He gave up His spirit [55]."

So, based on these verses I would allow for us to pray:

"Lord, Jesus, I come to you knowing I am unclean and far-deserving of your loving-kindness and mercy, and yet, Lord, have mercy on me and make me clean! I also know that because my sins have separated me from you for you, so I ask that you forgive me of my sins and make me whole. I thank you for the forgiveness of my sins, for loving me so much you died on a cross where all of your word was 'finished!' Thank you Father, for sending your son to die for me, in my place as I can't save me from me. Lord Jesus, come into my life so I may have and find life in you!"

    Now that you have prayed this you are a Christian. The best place for you to get more information and to get into studying God's word is a local Church that's close to you. I also praise the Lord, our Savior, for your new life in Him.

Notes

Introduction

[1] John 3:17
[2] Galatians 3:19-25
[3] Romans 10:5, 13
[4] Romans 10:14-21

1 The Righteous and the Unrighteous

[5] Luke 15:1-2
[6] Matthew 9:12
[7] Mark 2:17
[8] Luke 5:31
[9] Ezekiel 33:9
[10] Isaiah 53:3
[11] Deuteronomy 33:29
[12] Isaiah 1:21
[13] Matthew 23:37; Luke 13:34
[14] John 4:10
[15] Matthew 9:6
[16] Isaiah 7:14; Matthew 1:23; Luke 1:31
[17] Hosea 11:1; Matthew 2:15
[18] Jeremiah 31:15; Matthew 2:18
[19] see Leviticus 10:9, as John abstained from drink: Luke 1:15
[20] Malachi 4:5; Isaiah 40:3; Luke 3:4
[21] 2 Kings 1:8; Matthew 3:4
[22] Psalms 40:7-8; Matthew 3:15
[23] Deuteronomy 8:3; Matthew 4:4
[24] Psalms 91:11-12; Matthew 4:6
[25] Deuteronomy 6:16; Matthew 4:7
[26] Numbers 23:3; Matthew 4:8; Luke 4:5

[27] Deuteronomy 10:20; Matthew 4:10
[28] see Psalm 22:18; Matthew 27:35; Mark 15:24; Luke 23:34; John 19:24
[29] see Zechariah 12:10; Psalm 22:16; John 19:18, 34-37
[30] Genesis 17:1-8
[31] Genesis 21:1-7
[32] Genesis 22:1-18, bold highlights mine
[33] John 15:15
[34] Romans 5:10

2 In Search of what's lost

[35] Luke 15:3-4
[36] Luke 15:8
[37] Luke 15:11-16

3 Rejoicing Over what's found

[38] Luke 15:5-7
[39] Luke 15:9-10
[40] Luke 15:17-24
[41] John 3:19
[42] John 10:14-18

4 The Proud Son

[43] Luke 15:25-32
[44] Matthew 23:13-31
[45] Matthew 23:34-36
[46] 2 Chronicles 24:20

5 The Unjust Steward

[47] Luke 16:1-3
[48] Luke 16:8-9; Expanded Bible
[49] John 8:37-47

6 Lovers of Money

[50] Luke 16:14-18

7 The Rich Man and Lazarus

[51] Luke 16:19-31
[52] 1 Corinthians 10:13

Call to Repentance: A Prayer for Salvation

[53] Luke 5:12, 13
[54] Luke 5:17-26
[55] John 19:30

ABOUT THE AUTHOR

Benjamin H. Liles is a freelance writer, poet, singer/songwriter teacher, blogger and Apologist. He also takes a good deal of time to ensure he gives the best and most adequate information as he is able according to the riches in Christ Jesus. He lives in the Texas Hill Country with his wife, Tanya (a talented graphic designer), and their two cats. He also maintains his own blog which can be found at http://www.benheliles.com.

Made in the USA
Coppell, TX
19 February 2026